Home Grown Wisdom

Features a Variety of Stories

Living in the USA (Freedom?)

Tennis Bum

Thirteen Siblings Plus

Mom

Driving School Kids II

Bonus Feature: K-Kids

Home Grown Wisdom

This book will hopefully remind you of your own past and everything you gained from it. Notice; that I did not say gained or suffered from your past. I believe you can only gain from your past. This is wisdom, it is Home Grown Wisdom.

This is not a lesson book but a book of real stories that will hopefully reflect to your past. We tend to look back on stories that made a difference to late in life. We should always reflect on the past, but not live in it, and acknowledge what we learned.

Wisdom is a deep understanding and realizing of people, things, events or situation, resulting in the ability to choose or act to constantly produce the optimum results with a minimum of time and energy.

Wisdom is also the comprehension of what is true or right coupled with the optimum judgment as to action.

Sophia

Personification
of
Wisdom

Home Grown Wisdom

This Book Is Dedicated To My Mother and Father
My Brothers and Sisters

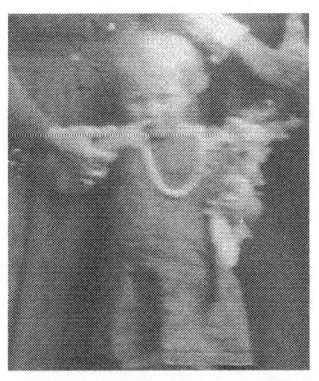 

Gretha (Janssen) Bojanac

Born In Oldenborg, Germany
1923-2004
Born, 13 Children

Daniel "Pop" Bojanac Deaushan

Born in Ugoslavia
1915 - 1988

The follow photos are all siblings in order of birth.

Home Grown Wisdom

Kathe Janssen
Born In Germany 1944

John (Yonk) Bojanac
Born In Germany 1946

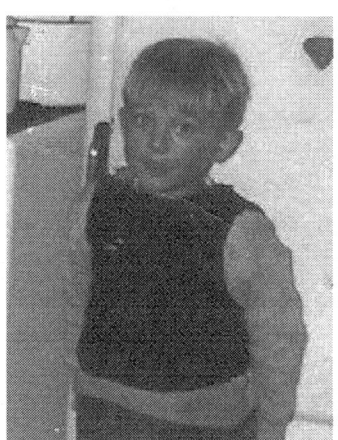

Paul (Pud) Bojanac
Born in Germany
1947

Pete Bojanac
Born and Passed in
Germany 9 Months old
1949-1949

Home Grown Wisdom

Pete Bojanac
Born in Germany
1951-1990

Amelia (Lubie) Bojanac
Born in America
1952

Danny Bojanac
Born in America
1954-1960

Bill Bojanac
Born in America
1955

Home Grown Wisdom

Mike Bojanac Born in USA
1956-2003

Gerald Bojanac Born in USA
1959

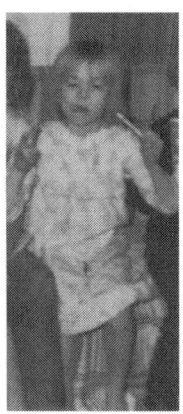

Janet Bojanac Born in USA
1960

David Bojanac Born in USA
1962

Home Grown Wisdom

Betsy Bojanac
Born in America
1963
13Th Child Born
By Gretha Janssen Bojanac

Home Grown Wisdom

Home Grown Wisdom

Subdivisions to **Home Grown Wisdom**

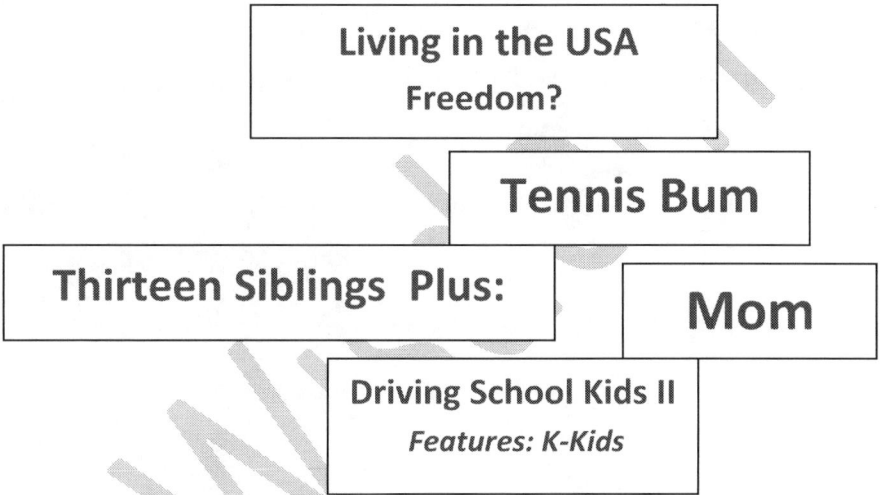

At the end of each chapter will be an analysis of Wisdom learned from the stories written; thus Home Grown Wisdom.

There will also be shared wisdom posted in a graphic called Shared Wisdom... These are testimonials of people who wanted to share wisdom they learned

Shared Wisdom

"I have an argument everyday with somebody." Bailey said. "I can never agree with anybody for any reason." "I'm sure I'm right most of the time but I don't know how to get past the need to argue." Bailey continued.

"I've been pushing my family away because I'm tired of arguing with them." "They and most people don't live my life and when they comment about it I get uncomfortable and stand up for my beliefs."

"Wisdom has taught me; it is never worth it to argue unless you have to win a case in front of judge, but I can't apply the wisdom in time to stop me from getting in an argument." Baily kept talking with confusion starting to set in. "I know what I'm saying but maybe my stubborn way I've learned is holding me back." "I want to be a peaceful person and just take things in without feeling like somebody is attacking my core."

Home Grown Wisdom

Directory

Living in the USA
Topic: Freedom?

Tennis Bum
Tennis Walls
Dream Racquet
First Tennis Match
Summer Tennis
High School Tennis
College Tennis
In The Army Now
Marching On
Dressed Like a Bum
Motorcycle Cramps
NAACP Tournament
Playing a Girl
Looks Can Be Deceiving
Bad Boy OF Tennis

Thirteen Siblings Plus

Mom
Gretha Bojanac

Driving School Kids II
Features K-Kids

Wisdom: Living in the USA
Topic: Freedom?

The freedom in America is short lived. Let's start from the time a person becomes an American, either from birth or immigrated to this country. We are all American's.

The freedom of life is preached to us and sold as the best thing America has to offer because no other country has the freedom we have.

We the people of the United States are controlled in every aspect of the word therefore the freedom that is said we have is only propaganda. Other countries use propaganda but they live up to it and don't try to falsify their actions with the word freedom.

From the time of birth we are monitored with a social security number. The number is your identity for the rest of your life. It will let the government or an authority institution know where you are every day of every year. It will also report your income and hold you responsible to pay the people who watch you so you conform to the western way of life.

When we are given the freedom to drive a vehicle we are controlled by speed limits and watched by police and now video cameras are everywhere on the roadways. We are also given an age restriction of when we can start driving and when we get to old to drive.

When you get your license you do feel a sense of freedom. People do feel the freedom with the need to drive as fast as they can and most people believe they have the freedom not to obey the rules of the road.

All different ways of our freedom is controlled in every aspect of life, so are the ways you drive a car. If you don't do as posted by road signs, or obey the laws of the road you can spend many years in jail.

We do get the freedom to get an education in our many different structured school systems, but we find out that our country can't compare to other countries when it comes to learning. So the freedom to get the best education in the world isn't even offered in most of our schools. However if you can pay for the education you can have the freedom to go to the schools that can do just that. Since our schools are poorly funded by the government the education needed to obtain the highest amount of freedom is lost. You can obtain more freedom from being educated.

The reason you can get more freedom from being educated is: you have the knowledge to defend yourself at all times in all situations. If you know your rights or how to work within loop holes your level of freedom rises.

If you are an average citizen with an average income you get an average education. Yes, you do have a better chance to obtain a student loan from the government; however when you think about how long it will take you to pay it off will make you think twice. The government has that grip on you and there is no way to ever default on that money. However the government will let you default on other money you owe to other people through a program called bankruptcy.

When the government gives us the freedom to drink alcohol we are again controlled by them. We can't go out in public intoxicated or appear drunk because that's public intoxication. We can only drive a vehicle with a small amount of alcohol in our system.

Home Grown Wisdom

There are tons of other drugs circulating in the USA other than alcohol but the limited freedom to do drugs like pot is far removed from our society because we don't have freedom. Alcohol appears to do more harm to people yet the government choses what freedom they give us and how much of it.

Every dollar that we are so proud to earn is practically taken away from us. The taxes are for government spending. Our money, is spent on what they feel makes the country a better and stronger place for us, at least that is what is told to us.

We are given the freedom to work for whatever company, business. Our freedom is taken away from rules those employees's have. Rules and regulations can be so extreme at some work places that one would feel like they're working for the castapo in Germany.

We all know by now that the government takes our money and uses a lot of it for crazy programs or give it to the people who got them elected. We are told we have the freedom to voice our opinion as to where and how they use that money, but that doesn't work.

The freedom of speech is probably the best seller this country has going. The best example is when you hear hard core wrappers say the craziest things imaginable. If you think you have the freedom to curse like them out in public or call people derogatory names; go ahead and try it. You will be prosecuted for abusive language or defamation of character.

How about the right to bear arms? The freedom to carry a gun makes you feel powerful until you have to use it. Go ahead and use that gun for self-defense and see what freedom is taken away. See what happens to you if you lose that gun and don't report it. See what happens to you if somebody else uses your gun and kills somebody.

How about the freedom to have healthcare? The cost of healthcare if you can afford it is a major crime that is played out in our society everyday on television and right in your own home. The health care companies have the freedom to accept you or not, you don't have the freedom to choose them and keep them.

Don't you love the freedom you think you have to live where ever you want to live? I don't know about you but I'm living in segregation because of the income that comes into my house. I just would like to see the freedom to be able to move up to the top of the hill if I would like.

Home Grown Wisdom

You do have freedom in the USA, but it's limited and controlled. Of course we don't want a society out of control but we don't want to be told go enjoy these freedoms when they are not freedom at all. Freedom is: the right to do or say what you want without anyone stopping you, the permission to use something without restriction.

Our country looks at most things the people can do in the USA, as freedom of choice, but how far can you go? Go to Amsterdam and smoke pot; go to Germany and drive as fast as you want on the autobahn. Go to China or any Asian country before you go to college and get an education that will qualify you for any college.

When you go to these countries watch what you say and how you say it because most countries won't tolerate ignorance, at least they're up front about it. Some countries give everyone full healthcare, it comes out of your wages, but at least they have it.

Is this all just wishful thinking to have a socialist country where everybody has the freedom to live the same? Everybody wants to be driving that Porsche 120 mph, smoking those Cuban cigars and marijuana sticks, going home to an in ground swimming pool.

Poor people would like this lifestyle but the rich people would never allow us that freedom.

The Wisdom Learned here:

Just because we fall into idealism like believing we live in a free country compared to most, we still can live a good life. However we live our lives we can't get caught up into, your rights versus their rights, or I should have what he has. Your freedom is limited and the wisdom you get from that is frustration if you dwell upon it.

You have to live your own life and be respectful to yourself foremost. Don't hate on others because they have something you don't. Believe in fate and that everything happens for a reason and you'll find out those reasons soon enough.

Just love yourself and respect the fact that everybody, lives life with problems. And remember the next time you say you have the freedom to do something, you think about everything that comes with that freedom if you chose to use it

Home Grown Wisdom

Shared Wisdom

"I always associate wisdom with smart people, the Harvard type people." Bob said. "A person like me who works nine to five and my only concern is providing for the family, doesn't have time to apply wisdom; at least with the intent to use it."

"Many times I can look back on decisions I've made and know that something somewhere in time taught me enough to make a good decision." "That's wisdom, I suppose?"

I wish I did have the time to apply more wisdom into my life but, from what I understand making a good rush decision sometimes is based on wisdom learned." "I don't ever say I'm going to do this because that is the best way, or that would be a way somebody else did it and it worked out." " I usually just do it."

"The best wisdom I got is not to pressure myself with wisdom and just go through life doing the best I can when I can."

Home Grown Wisdom

David Bojanac
Tennis Bum

Niece T_____ from left,
Nep___ w___ ___ d their
friends after a ___sson

Preface: To Tennis Bum

A <u>Tennis Bum</u> lives in all of us.

We grow up learning many things in life, something's stay with us daily, and something's become memories. This is part of **Home Grown Wisdom**.

We find passion in only a few things in life, and most of the time we define our character out of what passions drove us to be what we are today. One passion was playing tennis.

Home Grown Wisdom

What ever defined your character, whether it be a sport like tennis, or music, or a job career you chose that guided you; you should step outside the box appreciate what made you. You will also see that you were influenced by more than what you do on a daily basis.

I was greatly influenced by tennis. I don't know why I was driven to play tennis but somehow it was there for me. Not just the game influenced me, but what was around the sport that gave me an appreciation for life.

We develop our character around every life's situation we're put in. The stories that came with playing tennis became a story worth telling. I'm sure as you read on; your own life's stories will come back to you. Hopefully you will also see that you do have a tennis bum in you.

If you like human interest stories, this is a good one.

Home Grown Wisdom

Tennis Bum

Tennis Wall's

Ball after ball after ball, no matter how many times the ball was hit that ball kept coming back. The ball would return from different angles, speed, and with different types of spins. It was hard to win. The wall was too good.

The ball would hit the wall on the side of my red brick house for hours. There was a pounding noise inside the house but nobody ever complained.

"David spends hours, hitting that ball against the house." Gretha, (my mother) said. "I hear him sometimes at seven in the morning." "He must really like doing that." My mother never complained about anything I ever did, she was the most passive yet supportive person anyone could imagine.

When it rains or snows a walk across the highway to the tunnels that were located by the river was always a great place to hit balls. There was an arch shape tunnel and a square shaped tunnel. The arch shape tunnel was the best. There was more room to move and you could hear the cars and trucks approaching from a further distance. Getting out of the way of vehicles was easier in this tunnel.

That echo sound in that arch tunnel was amazing. Singing and hitting the ball was always enjoyable to do. The sound of the bounces was used as a metronome to keep rhythm with the songs that was sung. The reverb and the exaggerated pitches created in the tunnel became a perfect sound studio.

A neighbor friend Bobbie was a great singer. She quite often came over to the tunnels. She usually would tell me she just was there to watch tennis being played against the wall. She would walk around kicking stones then sing shyly under her breath until I started our favorite song together, Lionel Ritchie's, duet, Endless Love.

Many other songs were sung but that was the money song for us. While I hit the ball inside that tunnel wall, singing that song ten or twenty times was normal for us.

The tunnels were ten feet from the river bank and if the ball came off the wall awkwardly there sometimes was a chance for it to roll right into the river. There were cracks throughout the tunnel and the ball often would hit those cracks creating a funny bounce and return angel. This was one aspect of the game that latter came in handy; being quick on your feet keeping the ball out of the river.

Automobile traffic was more prevalent during the summer months. Boat owners would come through to launch their boats at the marina that was nearby. Boat owners would drive by everyday and wave or stop and say, keep it up kid; someday you might be a pro.

Friend's knew where they could find me and often enough they would come and get me to play football or baseball. I would keep my racquet and ball with me just in case I wanted to go back and hit some more balls off the tunnel wall.

Dream Racket

Twelve years old was when I started hitting the ball against the wall. It was then when the dream tennis racquet arrived at a department store.

When the knowledge of the great professional tennis player Jimmy Connors used this racquet, the desire to have it got intense. Jimmy was ranked number one for 160 consecutive weeks using this type of racquet, from 1974-1977.

The T2000 Wilson tennis racquet was a pot of gold. Looking at that racket in admiration with the wire's that held the strings and head together and then the price tag made me wondered if I would ever own one.

The price tag for a boy that lived in the projects with a huge family in tow and a mother on fixed income whom worked two jobs was only a dream.

Admiring that racket was the only thing that could be done. Using the wooden rackets that was given to me by my brother Pete was the reality.

Pete gave me rackets that had professional tennis players names on them like, Poncho Gonzalez, and Jimmy Connors. I didn't know any better but those rackets were also as good as gold, because of who gave them to me.

That T200 was still a dream when spring hit after a cold winter. The tennis bug came early and hit this tennis bum hard that season. I was finally asked to play a real game of tennis. Mentally prepared and all the rules learned; it was time. Imagining me hitting the ball back to a person instead of the wall was finally going to happen.

Home Grown Wisdom

The challenge by a neighbor family friend, whom I idolized because of his great ability in all sports, created frenzy in me to get that WilsonT2000 because I thought I would play better with it.

The first opponents name was Rick, I called him Ricky and he called me Davey. Ricky was an all star in many sports in high school. He was the greatest short stop baseball player our high school has ever known. He also was a leading scorer on the basketball team and just the thought of playing him was overwhelming.

The focus on a new racket was in order so the attempt to keep up with this kid's talent could be met. The knowledge of his talent in tennis was unknown, but he assured me he was talented in all sports. The threat of a good beating was followed by his comments.

My focus became more intent to get that T2000.

I was told by a neighbor friend in the projects to go to the store and change the price tag on the racquet to the amount of money I could get together. In a desperate effort I took her advice.

Home Grown Wisdom

At the store a price tag was found that could be afforded, the change of the tags took place. The racquet was taken to the register and I ended up being twenty-five cents short.

The cashier was asked to hold the racquet for one minute because the project lady friend who told me to change the price tag walked in the store. The quarter was retrieved and the cashier was paid and out the store I went. While jumping on the bicycle, the store security grabbed me and took me into the manager's office.

Shock hit and just steering at the monitors that watched the customers walk about the store was all there was to do. We waited and waited for the police to arrive as well as my brother Pete.

While waiting and watching the security monitors, my observation of the lady from our projects filling her purse with socks and underwear was going on. The awareness of crime hit me and the shock started wearing off as I began to realize what I did. This would be the only time this situation would play out in this life.

Home Grown Wisdom

After weeks of mental torture of what might happen to me was brutal. I had to pay a fine and pay for that racquet times ten. Of course my brother Pete was there as he always seemed to be for support. Pete was also the person whom brought me the racquet from the magistrate's office with words of advice.

Ricky waited and the day to play the first real tennis match was here.

First Tennis Match

From the time a scheduled match was talked about to the time it was actually played was nearly two months. Tennis ceased after the episode dealing with the crime with the T2000, no tennis against the wall or anywhere else. The embarrassments of those actions were overwhelming.

The thought of never picking up a racket again was considered. When the fine was paid off and the store got their money for the T2000, my brother Pete brought home the racket and said, "Only remember this period in your life as a one time event; now get out and play some tennis."

That racquet was held with mixed emotions. The racquet immediately was brought to the bedroom and was placed on the book shelves. While lying down on the bed an empty stair overtook the moment as sleep hit. The memory of waking up after falling to sleep and then seeing the T2000 on the shelf was a moment of joy. Jumping out of bed and grabbing the racket and holding it close to the heart was awesome. The racquet became a guardian angel, because it was a symbol of life's lessons.

The T2000 was finally a prize possession. With the make shift tennis bag, (a book bag), a run to the tunnel was in order. Hitting those tennis balls brought out anger and then happiness. There was so much energy the wall took a beating all night.

Getting use to the first metal racquet and its amazing pop on the ball took some time. This racquet was something special because of better control of where I wanted to aim the ball. The feeling of a professional started to creep into the body and the wall had no chance that day.

Later that evening a trip to a friend's house was scheduled. While walking through our town Ricky was spotted talking to his friends. After running to him the burst of, "ready to play" come belting out. He joked then had words of intimidation. Those words

Home Grown Wisdom

meant nothing to me, because only the thoughts of playing a human being instead of a wall were center focus.

The next morning was here and walking to Ricky's house or even getting dress wasn't remembered. Ricky's grandma was watching the early morning price is right on television. After watching the show for a few minutes I asked grandma to have Ricky go to the tennis courts when he awakes.

There was a wall along the way and hitting the ball many times was a good warm up. While walking the railroad tracks the rest of the way eating berries and wild apples gave me that breakfast that was forgotten.

Ricky finally showed up a little late. He was a prime athlete so he spent a good half hour stretching. The minutes became hours. Then Ricky's friends noticed him on the courts and before you know it we had an audience. Now there was intimidation and fear setting in.

Home Grown Wisdom

We started hitting the ball and the balls that came off the T2000 were long and wide, there was no control. Many adjustments started taken place as Ricky's friends made remarks about our poor play. Then finally they left and Ricky said relax and the game would come to me.

That's all it took. I actually had game.

We played long and hard. Friends would come by and watch for awhile but that no longer bothered me. A tennis match was finally being played with me in it, and boy I loved it.

No thoughts of winning or losing occurred until Ricky called out the score. The first set was lost and Ricky somehow was on the losing point of the second set. The second set was finally won. That point and time was when a realization of a set won by me was brought by incredible joy.

Ricky turned on his athletic skills and did not let another game slip by him. I didn't need to win the match that day because I couldn't get over the fact I could play good tennis. The over joy of love of this new sport was taken place. I was a tennis bum.

While walking the main street of our home town with a smile a mile wide, I waved to friends and neighbors as being in a victory parade. A school teacher stopped me and he said he watched a little bit of the tennis match. He said to keep playing because he thought I had a lot of talent on the tennis court.

When arriving home cleaning that new racket was the first thing that had to be done. The T2000 was laid on the bed with a big kiss. A prayer of thanks was spoken and then reminiscing about the match that was just played took over.

Every point kept playing in the mind, every second was played back as a smile was beaming across my face. There was no understanding of my new found love but nothing was going to replace it.

Summer Tennis

Now a young teenager with a passion for tennis, that's alien to most, playing where ever and whenever was always in order. Ever since that first match with Ricky many people asked to play. The true talents in sports in the town must have gotten wind that Davey was good at tennis.

I probably only won a few matches out of hundreds this first year but it never mattered; just playing tennis was too much fun.

Winter came but the racket stayed close to the bed. Bouncing balls off the strings to keep a feel of the racquet and game in my mind was something done every day.

The next summer didn't come soon enough. Ricky had a passion for tennis also so we played early spring in the rain and in the

Home Grown Wisdom

winters last few snow falls. Passerby's quite often yelled at us. The comments inspired more energy to play harder.

The end of school was here and a choice of whether to stay in Pennsylvania for the summer or go to California was troubling me. California was a place that was often dreamed about.

With in the first two days of arriving in California, the T2000 and I were playing tennis. From that day until the last day in California tennis was played every morning for six hours. A break at home, swim in the pool was how the down time was spent. Night tennis for at least four hours followed. The courts were always filled but waiting never was a bother.

The opportunity to play with some outstanding tennis players was the most beneficial aspect of going to California. The extra play in constant good weather took my game to a new level I never thought existed. A new style of play also came with it.

Bjorn Borg was the idol. The long hair with a sweat band around the head and the tight white tennis shorts was followed to a tee. His style of tennis, lobbing and ground strokes that had a lot of top spin was also worked into my game.

The look of a California surfer was also mirrored.

The summer in California was over and the trip back to Pennsylvania with a very dark tan and long blonde hair had the friends wondering what kind of summer I had. Mental and physical changes happened over the summer; I was also engulfed with Bjorn Borg's tennis vibe.

High School Tennis

The posting for signups at the school for the boy's tennis team was in full sight. I couldn't sign up out of fear. I later went to Ricky's house and told him about my fears. He threatened to kick my ass if I didn't sign up.

Home Grown Wisdom

Joining a team was intimidating so I put it off to the final day to sign up. When talking to my brother Pete about this dilemma, he asked me. "Will you be happy if you don't play?" I said, "Definitely, no!", and then he changed the subject.

The tennis team had its first meeting. The head coach pulled me aside and said, "If you want to play on his team a haircut has to be done." He then said, "You look like a bum."

Brother Pete was later informed on what the coach said. There was no way this hair was going to be cut because Bjorn Borg has long hair. Pete asked, "Does it really matter if you have long or short hair to play tennis?"

The next day at practice with the tennis attire and long blonde hair the walk of a proud Bjorn Borg look alike walked onto the courts. The coach didn't say anything directly to me but addressed haircuts and grooming in the following meeting.

"We are a team, and we wear the same uniform, and we groom ourselves to look like tennis players and that's the way it is or

Home Grown Wisdom

you're not part of the team." The day was over and the thought of a hair cut entered the mind but it never happened.

The next day at practice while walking onto the courts the coach called me over and tried to embarrass me in front of the other players. "Why don't you look like a tennis player Bojanac?" he yelled. "I do look like a tennis player, coach; I look like the greatest tennis player that ever lived, don't you think so?" I replied.

The coach's favorite player wasn't Bjorn Borg so it took him awhile to catch on. When he did, he sent me to court three to play doubles. The team spirit was now in me. That evening after practice the hair was cut down to a preppy style.

"Bojanac!" the coach yelled. "What the hell are you doing now?" "You went through all of my abuse and then I accept you for following in your idol's footsteps, then you cut your hair." "Why?"

The feeling of being a tennis player was all that was needed. The feeling of being your own self out on the tennis court and in day to day life was the answers.

Home Grown Wisdom

College Tennis

No tennis team at the junior college, but they had intramural tennis tournaments. The winner of these tournaments was reviewed by the athletic department that gave recommendations to the University.

Not knowing there was scouting going on during these events, my play wasn't intense, however the drive to play hard was always aroused by people watching. The unknown scouts only watched a few points out of everybody's match.

One day while relaxing in the dorm, my door was pushed open and another tennis player yelled, "You better get your butt up to the courts; your match begins in ten minutes." With no clean cloths and trying to get rid of a hangover from the night before, off I ran.

While running with another fellow tennis partner; he informed me that a few University scouts were at the courts and that the match I was playing was the only one scheduled.

After getting to the courts and looking at the most people I ever seen in the stands I realized this could be that chance I needed to get a scholarship and move on to the University.

Home Grown Wisdom

First set lost 6-0. The second set was going to start and a scout walked over and asked, "Is that the best you got?" I stood up and ran to the nearest outdoor bathroom and threw-up. While walking back to the court I noticed the scout getting in his car. "Where you going, you haven't seen anything yet?" "Come on, you'll enjoy this." I yelled.

Second set won 6-0. The third set was about to start and the same scout came over and said, "You got it kid." While he was talking, the hang over took over. Running back to the bathroom and getting sicker by the second the third set was cancelled.

While at the hospital a sexually transmitted decease was being discussed by the doctors. After receiving a few shots that were very potent; the next few days were history.

Heading to class on my first day back, a stop at the mail box was always necessary. A lot of coffee talk and gossip was always fun to partake in. While reaching into the mailbox I heard the tennis opponent from the week before yell, "I can't believe they accepted me on the tennis team at the University." My hand came out of the mail box empty.

I saw that same tennis player in the quad and asked if he was free to play a match. We played and I won 6-0, 6-0. There was only him and I at the courts, no scouts.

The second year at the junior college I traveled with every sports team because of the job I held as Sports Editor of the newspaper. We were at the University many times and quite often running into the tennis player that got the scholarship happened.

He said he was doing great every time we ran into each other. He said he made the second doubles team and was playing a lot.

When getting the first newspaper from the University from the mailbox my roommate pointed out that his name wasn't on the tennis roster. In that same paper, and the only article of concern, was information about upcoming tryouts for the University tennis team.

Home Grown Wisdom

Most of the past month was spent reporting on sporting events instead of playing in them. The body was out of touch so many good work outs was in order.

The gymnasium was open until ten o'clock every night. After my last class for that day I spent every second I could in there and did this for two weeks straight.

Tryouts were bright and early one Saturday. The weather in the mountains during the morning is always cold or cool, and this morning wasn't an exception.

Breakfast in the cafeteria was mostly leftover food from the prior week mixed into an omelet. The chocolate milk from the metal cow was always a favorite and drinking several glasses was never a problem.

Sitting in a classroom after a big breakfast and lots of chocolate milk was the norm except for this morning, I had to play tennis.

Home Grown Wisdom

A few words of advice to athletes; don't drink chocolate milk from a metal cow in the schools' cafeteria before playing your sport.

Winning that match was difficult however; the opponent drank just as much chocolate milk and looked just as horrific. Neither person was picked to play at the University.

The last month of junior college a letter was placed in the mail box that read; David Bojanac, please attend the tryouts for our tennis team...The only other words remembered was the date and time and place.

That morning of another tryout was here and sitting in a cafeteria at the University instead of the Junior College, felt awkward as I stared at the chocolate cow.

The breakfast was perfect; real fruits of all flavors, prime juices, wheat bread and sweets that made your eyes water. The feeling of just getting off a deserted Island and finding paradise was in the thought process.

That food was good and plentiful and took the thoughts away from having to compete for a tennis spot on the University team.

The courts didn't have outdoor bathrooms; they had a huge building with all the amenities and that's where most of the time was spent. What happened? No chocolate milk was ingested.

This match went 7-6, 7-6 in the lost column. This match was against the same opponent that took the spot in the first tryouts. The cards was working for him, however he never did see time on the University tennis team, and neither did I.

In The Army Now

No tennis in basic training. Not even time to think about tennis during this time in the army. The thirty mile hikes and gas chambers filled all thought capacity. However there was one evening when the fellow soldiers asked me to tell them a story before we went to sleep.

Being a squad leader during basic training had many peculiar moments. In the evening, the guys would ask me to sing a song or tell a story. This particular night was all about reminiscing about tennis.

It was a very hot summer morning, nearly ninety five degree's and being on the tennis court with no clouds above was treacherous. Looking across the net was one of the city's best tennis players for many years.

Twice the age he ran circles around men much younger than himself. The heat was in his favor, for it gave those old joints some type of lubrication. His approach to the game was also favored by playing in heat. In-between points he would walk real slow while you would be standing on the other side of the net sweating in the sun and heat.

Home Grown Wisdom

Many matches were played together but this one was unique in itself. Never beaten the man before, I none the less tried my best in every attempt to do so.

It was always a close match but when it came down to the serious points he knew just what to do to win them. Love forty in my favor and somehow he would always make it deuce and make me work even harder to win that game.

The first set was complete in two hours with the score 7-6 in his favor. (Three sets take that amount of time.) After the first set he sat in a chair that he brought and I sat in mine. I would jump up and want to get playing after a few minutes but he had other things in mine.

My opponent left the courts and went to his car for nearly twenty minutes. In that time I found a tree close by and sat under it. When he came back he had a new tennis outfit on and a new cooler with ice cold drinks.

Home Grown Wisdom

The second set lasted a little longer but ended with his loss 7-6. During the break of this set my opponent left the court again and came back with another new outfit and a video camera. We recorded the third match.

The third match began with the camera attached high on the fence behind him. It felt like the pressure was on to perform because I knew somebody would watch this tape at a later date.

Each point was intense and long. Great shots came from both of us. There was total concentration until the sky's got cloudy and it began to rain. Then the tempo got faster only to complete the match.

The courts were somewhat wet but safe to play. We were in a crucial game. There was a chance for me to win if I broke his serve. Game set match point was here and he served the ball. The ball skid on a little water puddle on the court and it was an ace.

After many match points and game points we were back to another match point. Deep on the baseline the ball was hit high and wide, I raised my hands in victory and started to run to the net when I heard his yell," look up". A gust of wind blew the ball back onto the court and he won that point.

We worked the game back to match point and during this point another high lob was placed by him. With the rain getting heavier and the wind getting stronger I watched that ball every inch of the way. The ball reacted the same way. While running to the ball I tried to stop and slipped and fell on my back. The ball hit directly beside me. I didn't recover and lost that game.

Now in the tie breaker we decided to play out the whole game even in the heavy rain. When I had the serve I would squeeze the ball to drain the water. I noticed when he had the ball he would roll it in the puddles to absorb the water.

Finally the game, set, match point was in my hands again. I noticed my opponent cleaning his glasses, and stalling for time. He then yelled, "I can't see anything." "This is ridiculous, let's finish some other time."

Home Grown Wisdom

The thunder clouds and lightning were getting closer. I yelled back, "Match Point!" He still tried to stall for time so he could use the lightning and thunder as his excuse. I rolled the ball in the puddle and served it. The serve was the slowest of all time. I just wanted to land it in the service court and I did. The ball skid and never bounced.

After winning I ran to my tennis bag, gathered all my belongings with my chair and ran to my car. While sitting in the car my opponent took his good old time as he did when the sun was baking us.

"How did you like that story guys?" I asked the fifty guys in my barracks. Only one guy responded, "You're the best Bojanac, now sing me that one Elvis song you do every night." "That's the song that puts me out."

The next morning while eating chow a few guys told me they only heard the beginning of that story the night before.

Home Grown Wisdom

Basic training went fast and before you know it the time at Fort Carson Colorado was here. Playing tennis in Colorado was tough. Gasping for air after every point was constant.

Playing against the wall was best I could do for the first month until I met Sgt. Jones. He practiced his serve with hundreds of balls while I hit one ball against the wall until I asked if I could just practice hitting his serves back to him. When his name was asked he replied, "Simply Jones, call me Jones."

This man was a great tennis player and I told him that. He didn't know where or how to go about getting on the Army tennis team. Since I had connections with the people who knew how to process paper work, we guided him in the right directions. He said, "If I ever make it I'll thank you by pulling on my ear and saying simply Jones.

Sgt. Jones was playing in a professional tournament in Houston, Texas and he won the match. During his interview on

Home Grown Wisdom

ESPN, he looked in the camera and said I owe this to a guy in Colorado Springs. He pulled on his ear and said, "Simply Jones."

Company orders for a trip to South Korea for the rest of my tour came in. Tennis seemed to be taken a back seat, but my drive to play was still at the forefront of my mind.

I was the battalion commander's secretary and my days were long and hard. The commander often talked with me regarding my life and hobbies and one day set me up with a gentle man she new to play tennis.

While waiting at the forts tennis courts in Soul Korea, my opponent arrived. He was a small man with little to say except for; let's get started.

This man cheated more than he called shots good. After many bad calls I started questioning him. "What the hell are you doing? I said. "Are you blind, those shots were all in."

Home Grown Wisdom

Nothing fazed him. I got tired of questioning the calls so I gave up. I walked off the court and went back to my barracks.

The next day the commander asked me how the game went and I told her that I rather not talk about it. We went on with our day. She reminded me that I had to be in class A dress code because the General was stopping by today.

While sitting in the office we heard, "Officer in the room." We all jumped up and saluted. Our eyes were straight ahead until he said, "as you were". After sitting down I felt a tap on my shoulder. Turning around I went into shock. I've seen a lot of high ranked officers but this one was the tennis player from my last match.

"So, you're the secretary to the commander?" he asked. "Yes, sir, sorry sir, I mean I didn't know I was playing a General the other day sir." I fumbled for words. "Sgt. Bojanac." He said as he stared at me. "Thank you for the wonderful experience." "Do you want to play again?"

Home Grown Wisdom

We were off playing tennis within that same hour. While playing I notice him cheating again. When I would look across the net he would look back and relay the score that best fit his desire. I would just nod my head and turn and smile from ear to ear.

The first set was in his favor 6-4 while we rested on the bench by the courts. "You know Bojanac, if somebody cheats you out of something you better speak up." The General told me. "You'll be respected more as a man." "Do you get what I'm saying?" Of course, yes sir was in order.

The second set started and the General called a shot long when it was clearly in. "What do you mean it was long; you didn't even bother to turn around to see if it was out or in!" I replied with frustration. "There you go, get some balls Bojanac!" The General yelled at me. "Just remember that tone when you're talking to a General." And of course yes sir was in order again.

The match ended up with the General winning. The General then asked me to play on his volleyball team when the weather got bad. The team was all American Samoan's except for me. The team was the best in South Korea. When we weren't playing volleyball we would play a lot of doubles tennis together.

Marching On

After the years in the military, moving to a dream place like Los Angeles, California was a priority. However finding tennis players wasn't as easy as when it was in the 1970's when I visited.

Finding a steady player was difficult so entering tennis tournaments was the next option. Every tournament listed in the USTA Magazines for that area I entered. Playing tournament after tournament took its toll on the body and injury after injury occurred.

While warming up for this one particular tournament my racket was in the back had position and the body stopped moving.

The next moment was the scariest time ever imagined. No feeling in the legs.

After collapsing on the hot tennis court my thoughts were of me in a wheelchair the rest of my life. There was no feeling in my legs so I asked some people to carry my limp body into a shady area.

I sat there for about ten minutes when the opponent asked if this was a forfeit. I got frustrated that he asked and when he did my legs came back to life rather quickly.

The match played on and ended in my favor. The need to win my last game ever because of a chance of being paralyzed stayed in the thought process while playing.

Tennis started becoming less important and the lapse time of seven years went by without playing. Employment became a focus as the body started changing also. Slower and fatter was a process that I somewhat lost control of.

Home Grown Wisdom

Before you know it the last California earthquake changed my life. Sleeping in a tent in a field next to my semi collapse home for a month made the decision to go back to Pennsylvania very easy.

With a yard sale that pulled in $5,000.00, every personal possession was sold except for items that would fit into a Toyota Camry. With the car packed, the trip across country took ten days because of stops in states where there were friends. The trip was a mini vacation.

The friends in Phoenix Arizona knew how to cheer up a broken soul, and that was to get him out on the tennis courts and boy did we.

One person brought an uncooked egg with him to demonstrate the way you could cook outdoors in Phoenix, Arizona. The egg was cracked on the tennis court we didn't play on. While we set up to play tennis the egg began to cook.

Home Grown Wisdom

The heat was undesirable however we played on. No match, just volley play. There were times where there were six people on one court only to keep us from running in that extreme heat.

We lasted an hour at best. The water went quickly and the desire to play on lost its charm. We packed it up; stopped by the area we cracked the egg and noticed only an outline of the egg was present. It was like a crime scene with the body missing except this was an outline of an egg.

The friends that moved to Phoenix from Los Angeles said that was the first time they used those rackets since they moved there six years ago. The heat was always the reason for not wanting to play.

There was a friend in Taos, New Mexico that was on the mini vacation trip list. With a short stay of no more than a few hours the road trip continued. I would have stayed longer if he knew how to play tennis.

With a layover in Oklahoma in a four star hotel, tennis was screaming my way. There was even a tennis tournament going on at the hotel. I got to sign up but then realized a lot of pain in my rear end. The development of hemorrhoids took place over the course of the trip.

I couldn't even enjoy watching the matches being played. The pain was like a tennis ball trying to squeeze out the back of my ass. Sitting wasn't recommended and wasn't attempted.

Long hot baths in the hotel room was the only way to relieve the pain. The baths were great; laying in a huge tub with bubble bath watching tennis on TV. The bath was often drained and refilled until the tennis telecast was over.

Off and running; the next stop was Indianapolis, Indiana. When I crossed that state line a State Trooper pulled me over. I had a very hard time getting out of the car because the hemorrhoids came back with a vengeance.

"Did you know you were speeding sir?" The trooper asked. I was in so much pain I started crying. "I just lost my house in an earthquake, and then lost my job because the building got demolished, then I have to move back to Pennsylvania, and then I get hemorrhoids and now you're going to give me a ticket." I tried to tell the officer. "I guess I'm overwhelmed right now, I had the car on cruise control for the past hour."

"Ok." The officer replied. "Sorry to hear what you're going through." "I think I heard it all now." "It's all true, look I'll show you the hemorrhoid pillow that I just got at the pharmacy." I quickly said.

No ticket, only a warning. The office even told me that he would say a prayer for me and my hemorrhoids.

The stay in the hotel in Indianapolis lasted two days. Everything was tried to relieve the discomfort on my ass but little worked. The final leg of the trip had to be completed with all the discomfort. John Denver kept me positive as he sang on the CD player.

Home sweet home and three days in bed was all I needed with a lot of love from my mommy. While being home, more and more

Home Grown Wisdom

friends found out that I was in town and I began to get request to play tennis.

I would have settled for the tunnel by my old homestead but playing the boys that were now men had to be done.

A tournament in a nearby community was the event all the friends signed up for so a lot of practice was necessary. After that mini break I had to move on.

Double's was the only thing that was open in the age group that was sought. The only person available was a high school kid that was a friend of a friend whom didn't have anybody to play with.

With out ever practicing together, the team work and our ability to communicate was unbelievably great. He followed up on any mistakes I made and I followed up and corrected any mistakes he made.

Home Grown Wisdom

The final's in this tournament was a dream but never thought it would be playing a doubles match. We started out with a bundle of nerves and a few small ailments but they quickly disappeared.

The quality of the game was the best we ever played. A small group of people started watching the match. By the end of the first set the stands were filled.

Who ever knew that crowd support would be such a big adrenaline rush? When they applauded it gave me such joy that I found myself constantly smiling.

We won the first 7-6. We lost the second set 12-10. In the third set both teams were noticeable tired but we played hard because of the crowd. Neither team wanted to lose.

We were at match point and my team-mate got intense cramps. He told me to serve the ball and try to cover the whole court and I did. This lasted through many points. They got match point then we did many times.

Home Grown Wisdom

We asked for an injury time out and got one. This only made things worse. We got back on the court and the other team did everything to keep the ball away from me. I ran more and worked harder in that game than I did all set.

Deuce and Ad-in then Ad-out with my partner in extreme pain; we both wanted to end the game. At that point winning didn't seem important but somehow we played on.

We believe there were twenty deuces during that game and then it all fell apart. The court got too big to cover after several hours of playing and they broke my serve.

We made an effort to be competitive in the remaining points but fate wasn't with us that day. The crowd stood and cheered and I broke down and cried. That doubles match took a lot out of us. It gave us a lot of good memories and confidence that lasted a lifetime.

Home Grown Wisdom

Dressed Like A Bum

When doing any traveling, some of the tennis equipment and an outfit or two would travel with me. Going on a camping trip in the forest and taking tennis balls to juggle with was the closest I thought I would get to tennis.

Deep in the wooded forest were many areas to set up tents. The running water from a nearby creek and birds chirping was the only thing to be heard. Setting up camp was done in a hurry as we set up tents, gathered wood for fires and then decorated our own little sites.

While sitting around the fire that evening a few neighbor campers stopped by. We were drinking and eating and throwing tennis balls. One of the visitors told us that he was a tennis player and there was a tennis tournament in the village close by.

Before you knew it my entry was called in and the morning came quickly as the neighbor camper stopped by to pick me up.

Home Grown Wisdom

When walking to the car, nearly a mile away I realized that I only had a racket that I let the niece's and nephew's use. These racquets were taped up and old.

That was the period when withdrawal crossed my mind. My new tennis friend assured me that there would be racquets at the event for renting.

After renting the racquet we were in a dressing room. This was when it hit me that I had only the clothes on my back. Handkerchief on my head, a white T-shirt that had a few stains, cut off jeans and black socks with dirty tennis shoes was the outfit for the day.

I just wanted to play. Who would I know out in the forest so far away from home? I kept a low profile until my name was called to court one. The court that was closest to the restaurant and viewers.

How embarrassing it was to walk out on the court looking like a real tennis bum. Only a few people were present to watch so I played on with the constant thoughts of embarrassment.

Winning the first set easily and then the second, I was off the court in no time. Fifteen minutes later my name was called again to play on court number one. I thought I was done for the day. I was told this was a lumberjack tennis tournament and all games had to be played today.

Winning the second match in an hour's time made me think I had time to go wash up, but my name was immediately called again. There I was again on court one and the crowd started getting bigger and the restaurant was full.

My opponent was a gentleman that won every event on the east coast. I couldn't wait to lose. After winning that match because of default I was called to play again. You guessed it, on court one.

The finals...? How did I make it to the finals?

Home Grown Wisdom

I lost the last match in the finals and was sweating more than I ever have in the past. There was body odor that I thought was from a dead man, but it was mine.

While walking to the car we heard my name to report to court one. We returned to the courts and a trophy presentation was beginning. "He dressed the part and ended up short." The announcer said over the loud speakers. With embarrassment, the wood carved trophy was received and we hurriedly went back to camp late that evening.

I put the trophy by the camp fire and washed up and changed cloths. The other fellow campers were down at the water lighting fireworks.

While getting dressed they returned and sat around the fire. I told them about my adventure and we laughed and laughed. One person asked if I won anything and I replied a wood carved trophy. That was when everything got quiet.

A few people stood up and started walking away when one person started crying and saying, "I didn't know what that ugly thing was." "Who knew it was a trophy?"

The trophy added to the flames for several marshmallows roasting. The cloths that I wore were also added to the fire, for that story had to be forgotten.

Motorcycle Cramps

 The trip to the tennis courts was short and the weather was hot so the motorcycle was the choice for transportation. The tennis bag was strapped down to the back seat by bungee cords.

 Driving to the match felt a little chilly because the sun just started to break the horizon. A nice windbreaker help keep me warm as I drove on the parkways without stopping.

Home Grown Wisdom

The tennis courts were already filled with players so my opponent suggested driving to a nearby court. His version of nearby wasn't the same as mine, as I followed him for nearly twenty miles.

The courts we arrived at were also crowded except for one court. This court wasn't taken because of the cracks that ran all through it. There were even puddles of water that had to be dried up.

Playing the person that I played this day was a struggle in itself. He was known as the wall. He returned everything no matter where or how hard you hit it. You only hoped he returned the ball outside the lines.

This match like the matches we played in the previous year's lasted several hours. I learned tennis on the wall so I knew how to have patience with this type of player.

My strategy changes during the game several times when playing a pusher or a wall type of player. I love to come out and swing for the fences and put everything on the line. If the opponent

Home Grown Wisdom

is up for the challenge and defends all I got on that level I resort to another style of play.

This day we played my style for the first set and he won. Then we both became a wall. It wasn't pretty but I was in better shape and realized I would out last him.

The second set I won and we moved onto the final set. Again, I felt the need to swing for the fences and found myself down. The game plan changed and we continued with his style of play.

The four hours to finish three sets was over. There was nothing left in both of our body's. We talked as we gathered our tennis gear and once again he vowed to beat me next time we played.

I knew I had to keep my body moving so I ran to my bike that was basking in the sun. I used a towel to blanket the seat for a minute before I sat down and then quickly drove off in the summer sun.

Home Grown Wisdom

I made it to the city and while crossing over the river on one of many bridges, my body started cramping. My rib cage got immediate pain. I started breathing heavy and realized I had to get off the bike.

While on a four lane bridge with many cars and trucks I managed to get off the bike. Right in the middle of the lane I stood as I tried to stretch the cramps out. That is when a police officer pulled next to me and yelled, "Get on your bike now, and get off this bridge."

I struggled as the pain was intense. I managed to make it to a safe spot, a few yards from the police station. I walked around until I thought I could drive home. I then got cramps everywhere on my body after getting on the bike.

I got off the bike again and walked into a carpet store and asked for help. They thought I was a drug attic or something as they lead me to the door and told me to get out. I walked to the police station in a hunched position, gasping for air and then started crying for help.

Home Grown Wisdom

I rang the buzzer by the door and I tried to explain what I needed but they told me to go away. I kept ringing the buzzer until a police officer came out and started yelling at me.

I fell to the ground and begged for help. The officer told me that I had only a minute to get myself together before he arrested me. I looked up at him and told him to go to hell. He walked away and then I managed to crawl under a tree for shade.

I laid there for an hour and finally got my body to relax. I focused on breathing and being calm. There were times where the anxiety was too great but somehow I pulled through.

While driving home I passed that same police officer and I flipped him the bird and he then did the same to me. The cramps came back as soon as I parked the bike at home.

NAACP Tournament

This NAACP tournament was posted on every court that I played on that early spring. When there is a tournament I sign up, win or lose.

There are twenty six courts where this tournament was played. When I arrived for my scheduled match I noticed that only black people where playing tennis on every court. I was the only white person to be found.

I felt right at home. If I was driving through a neighborhood and noticed a basketball game going on I would stop and see if I could get winners. Nine times out of ten times I would be the only white person there also. So arriving at a tennis facility with all black people present wasn't awkward at all.

The only thing that was going through my mind as I carried my tennis bag past court after court then towards the sign in table was; I wonder if they knew I was white when they scheduled me. I also thought I was going to be turned away because I was white.

I arrived at the table and several people asked if I was there for the tournament. After saying I was, they directed me to the scheduling table where a panel of people was there to take all the information.

"My name is…" I tried to tell one lady. "You must be David Bojanac." "Your match starts in one hour on court thirteen." "Go to the next table to sign in and get your shirt." I had to ask what NAACP meant and then she told me. We awkwardly both laughed as she thanked me for entering.

One hour latter I was on court thirteen waiting for an opponent when I was called back to the sign in table. I had to wait for an additional hour. After that hour my opponent showed up, a white guy.

After beating him I was in the second round. I played a great match up to the point when I pulled a groin muscle. My opponent kept telling me to take as much time as I needed but I had to default.

I looked for the NAACP tournament the following year, but they moved the event. The travel time to go to that tournament was more than I wanted to deal with so unfortunately I didn't play.

Playing a Girl

The city has a tennis challenge ladder system that is coed. My first year on the ladder there were over two hundred players that signed up. There were nearly twenty females that also joined.

A match was schedule with a female who had a great record even against male players. She was on the local university tennis team.

Home Grown Wisdom

I was near the top of the ladder and she wanted the chance to advance over me so she pursued the game. Her schedule was tight and she only had a certain night and times to play me so we scheduled it.

It rained all day but we both knew it would stop an hour before we hit the courts. She called me and we worked out a plan to go up earlier than scheduled to dry off the court.

I arrived an hour early and took a squeegee and a few towels to dry off the court. Every court was soaking wet. It was night time so there was no sun to help dry it. I chose court thirteen because it looked like it had the best lighting and was an end court.

I spent that whole hour bent over drying that court before she showed up. The first thing she said was, "I am superstitious and will never play on court thirteen." The first thing I said was, "Here is a squeegee, go pick a court, and I'm taking a break."

Home Grown Wisdom

We started off on a bad note as we didn't say anything the entire time she worked drying the court. I helped a little but was worn out from clearing and drying court thirteen.

We started playing when puddles of water started appearing from under the courts surface. We ultimately moved to court thirteen.

This girl hit as hard as a man and had great angle shots that put me to the test. I was so confident I was going to win prior to playing that I didn't bring a new can of tennis balls that the winner gets. I had to win because I would have been embarrassed.

After losing the first set I told her that I didn't bring a new can of balls for her if she won. She replied, "Just give me five dollars." That statement gave me what I was looking for and that was an attitude.

I no longer felt I had to slow down my serve or hit my power forehand.   I let her have it. If she was at the net I drilled it right at her. This girl became public enemy number one.

Home Grown Wisdom

She lost the second set badly and commented during the break that I got lucky. That statement put me over the edge and my shots became Federer like.

She tried everything to break my maintained angered train of perfection but it did not work. She even tried to stop the match to reschedule because she said she got injured.

She finally gave in and played on only to go down in defeat. This was her worst loss ever. She could not bring it upon herself to congratulate me or even shake my hand.

A few days later I received an e-mail from her thanking me and congratulating me on my win. She was even apologetic. I responded with my own e-mail, thanking her for letting me find out that if I get a little anger in my system while playing I can play like Roger Federer.

Home Grown Wisdom

Looks Can Be Deceiving

Playing in a tournament in Colorado Springs, Colorado had its up's and down's. The weather is extremely unpredictable. One minute you could be enjoying the warmth of the sun and next minute it could be snowing on you.

This tournament was located by the Springs Airport. When arriving at the courts we were told that we had to wait for the sandstorm to be over with. We waited from 7 a.m. to 9 a.m.

Home Grown Wisdom

The winds were howling over sixty miles an hour. Many of the players got board standing around so we took turns to see who could run across the court without getting blown over.

Walking with the wind was easier than walking into the wind. After running to one side of the court you had to come back with the wind and sand hitting you full force. You would literally have to lean forward until you were almost in a prone position, almost in a pushup position.

The wind died down and the tournament was underway. My opponent met me at the sign up table and I wasn't sure if he wanted to wrestle me or tackle me. He was not built like the average tennis player.

My game plan came instantly to me. Make this big guy run until he falls over.

I got my ass kicked. I ran more than I ever did in a match. His serve was three times faster than the wind we had earlier. This man was faster than players I've played prior to this match.

Home Grown Wisdom

This was a double elimination tournament so I had another chance. The second match with a different player started around noon and we were then told a storm was coming in and we might be suspended for a period of time.

Ten minutes after we started playing a different type of storm raced over Pikes Peak and hit us full force. The hail was the size of tennis balls. They covered the courts within minutes. There was no attempt to run across the courts during this storm.

Just a fast as it arrived, it ended. The sun came out and quickly melted and dried off the courts and we began to play on.

After winning that match I was told to come back the next day. The next day we were hit with another wind storm but it didn't last as long.

I met my opponent at the sign up table and we walked to our court. I was playing the same big man I started the day before with. The story with this match was different. I always learn something playing a person the first time and this time around I used what I learned.

He was big, yes; He was fast, yes; He also had a big serve, yes; and he was a better player than me. What I got from all of this was I didn't have a chance in hell.

After winning that miracle match I had to review it in my mind several times. He clearing out played me but somehow I hung in there and won the big points.

While out on the court with the next match we were honored to witness the supersonic jet; the Concord landed at the nearby airport. We were all shocked by the supersonic boom and then we saw the plane fall out of the sky like it was out of control.

It heading right toward us and turned like it was a hovercraft and swiftly took off to the airfield. Everybody stopped play and we all just stared off into space like we just seen an UFO.

Home Grown Wisdom

Not more than ten minutes after the Concord landed snow began to fall. The snow storm lasted for twenty minutes and then began to rain. After the rain the sun came out. Twenty minutes after the sun came out it started snowing again.

I had a big day scheduled the next day so calling it quits on this tournament had to be done. The next day the big man that I played twice was in the local paper as being the winner of the tournament.

Bad Boy of Tennis

There was always an influential person in my life. At every crossroad or every milestone, the angels placed people in front of me to watch. Weather I listened to them on the radio or watched them on television I was guided by them.

My bother Pete was the most influential man in my life and I still reflect on him even today. After Pete died in a car crash I had to move on. I lost something great, but we were still together in spirit.

There were influences by good people and bad people. I had friends who were very wealthy to dirt poor. I always treated people with respect no matter what age or color. If you disrespected me, I would just walk away and remove you from my life.

If there was a bad person that was interesting to me with his or her ways of life then I would gravitate towards them. There was always a need to know why somebody would grow their hair long, or paint their hair blue, or cut up their cloths to create a different style.

Home Grown Wisdom

I was fascinated not only in the physical sense of people being interesting but with people's belief's. Why they might be an atheist, or a Catholic over a Protestant, or why they might be shy and then the next person outgoing.

I never wanted to be an atheist or convert my religion but I had the ambitions to grow my hair, wear different cloths or just try what the next person was doing.

On the tennis court there was Bjorn Borg for my look, but I admired John McEnroe for his fiery attitude for his belief in judgment calls on the court.

I was drawn into tennis even more win my heroes would play. They were so different in all aspects of life. Their lives were given to us by Television and we adopted those few hours that we would see them as their total life. We never thought that they could act different off the court.

Home Grown Wisdom

While playing an opponent whom I respected, then witnessing him calling shots that were good, no good, brought out the Mac Attack in me.

"What do you mean the ball looked out?" I yelled while approaching the net. "You know it was in." "Is that what I have to deal with the rest of the game?" "That was clearly in!"

This man got so embarrassed but then got caught up in the moment and started his rampage. When it was his turn to rage I just walked back to the baseline and motioned for him to play on.

He obviously got heated out of my reaction and played with more intense ground strokes. In between games I told him that McEnroe possessed my soul. He then joked and said he thought it was Eli Natasi.

This match had all the characteristics of a McEnroe match. I felt I was being cheated by several more calls and tried to hold my thoughts in but the Mac Attack serviced again and again.

Home Grown Wisdom

The tennis community is a small community and close friends told me to relax or people won't want to play you. The damage was done as only a few requests to play came my way. I had to change my reputation from a McEnroe to a Borg type of player.

This behavior change was hard to do as every match had controversial calls. I thought maybe I needed an exorcist to rid me of the Mac inside me.

I learned in time to bite my tong but that caused me to through my racket. When I broke my first racket I realized that I was too poor to buy a new one so that didn't last long.

My passion to win matches was overwhelming and I had the hardest time getting rid of the Mac attacks. Then peace came over me. I told an opponent one time that I saw the ball was good and he called it out, in a nice polite tone of voice. We talked about it and decided to replay the point.

This is the way my brother Pete would have told me to handle this situation, and I know he told me this in one way or another.

Home Grown Wisdom

Even after I realized that being polite was the correct way to handle a controversial call, I every now and then will bring back Mac just to get me fired up to win.

Dedication to John McEnroe: You were an amazing player. I was always fascinated with your antics and your tennis style of play. You appeared as a poor boy that made it big. I got this from your rugged look. Your hair was never combed and your socks were never pulled up. You were living the life I was supposed to have. I hope you enjoyed it.

Tennis Lessons

The wonderful thing about tennis is everybody can play the game. This was my opinion prior to giving lessons to a group of middle school kids and their parents.

When you're at the courts you see family's with the mom and dad and young kids hitting the ball. They're usually on the courts I'm playing at but none the less they are out there getting some exercise and enjoying the game.

Home Grown Wisdom

I was approached by a family that was watching the match I was playing. They told me that I had a great game and wondered if they could pay me to teach them how to play.

I volunteered my service because it was just a pleasure to be on the court, and now somebody trusts me to teach them. This was an honor to me.

We started immediately. I explained a simple drill I wanted them to try and they were enthusiastic to begin. This drill was only supposed to last five minutes. We got through one round of the drill after twenty minutes. I was exhausted and told them we had to schedule practice for another day.

We decided on the following day bright and early, because the family was on vacation. They offered again to pay me and I immediately accepted this time. I had to get something out of what I knew was going to be a trying experience.

The next morning I set the court up with orange cones for them to aim at and I had two jump ropes for conditioning. After explaining the two, they immediately said keep the cones and ditch the ropes.

The cones were also ditched after twenty minutes of trying to get the family to hit them. They complained that they were a distraction.

I placed the family up along the fence and asked only one person to be on the court at a time with me. I would hit the ball to this person and then they would hit it back. I asked them to rotate in and off the court as fast as possible.

The kids cut in front of the parents and the mother gave up after two rounds. She pulled me aside and asked me to just give her real tennis lessons instead of trying to kill her.

I asked the remainder of the family to move to another court while I focused one on one with the mother. I then told them I would rotate with each of them.

Home Grown Wisdom

Instead of moving to another court they sat on the bench and watched. I showed the mother the correct way to hold the grip on the racquet. She then had to swing at the ball using the forehand approach. After every coaching tip I gave, one of the family members not being coached would run onto the court and say, "Mom, this how you do it."

Not one member of this family had a clue as to what they were doing out there. I felt the best lesson I could give them was to watch them as a family and then correct them as they played.

Why did I think that would work? They felt I was interrupting their big moment as tennis professionals. "What do you mean?" "I hit that ball nice and hard." The father yelled at me. "Just because it doesn't hit inside the court doesn't mean it was a bad shot."

With that logic I stood behind the baseline to hit the balls they would miss only to keep the ball moving. I hit nine out of every ten balls that came over the net.

Home Grown Wisdom

The lesson was over and the mother tried to hand me forty dollars. I explained that I didn't do a good job and didn't deserve it. They tried to schedule another lesson but I told them my schedule was booked the rest of summer.

I see that family every now and then on the courts and they yell proudly. "Hey, there is our tennis coach." If I'm with friends I give a quick wave and move away as fast as possible.

Wisdom Learned:

If you have the desire to do something and need certain things to make it happen, use your head and think out the consequences before you do something criminal, like change a price to a racquet.

Always be true to yourself and try to achieve what you want in life but always enjoy the people along the way.

Find the right people in your life to make things happen. If you fail, get through the pain and gather yourself and move on. The best person and the only person you should rely on are yourself.

Shared Wisdom

"I've been married seven times and can't believe I wasted my time with idiots like those men." Katie said. "I don't want to get married again but I found me a new man who loves me."

"I'll just take it as it comes because I have other problems." "My own kids won't talk to me, I have a big family and I only talk to one or two of them." Katie kept talking. "They all say I'm the problem but I don't see how."

"How can these people treat me so wrong?" "I struggled most of my life and I get treated like shit." "They don't know me but they judge me." "And now you ask if I gained any wisdom from all this."

"Sure I gained wisdom from this; people are ignorant whether it be your own family." "I have to treat them like they treat me or they will win."

Preface to: **Thirteen Siblings.**

The pictures of the thirteen siblings are pictured in the first few pages of this book with our mother and father. Three generation spread in births played an enormous factor in living with this many brothers and sisters. Mostly because we all didn't get a good chance to know one another the way we could have.

What wisdom we got out of living with each other is still yet to be determined. As a family divided today, it seems like we learned very little, unless the decision of wisdom to stay away from one another is the right thing, then wisdom has served its purpose.

Growing up with this many siblings and relatives was more fun than one kid could imagine. Enjoy.

Thirteen Siblings

Plus:

The family managed on two crowded bedrooms with nearly a dozen kids most of the time. The phrase cheaper by the dozen was a misconceived concept. Cheaper by the dozen only meant each of us only got one if a dozen was supplied. It also meant we learned to create a dozen ways to manipulate any given situation.

How did we manipulate our situation with two bedrooms was somehow the easy part of living with at least twelve energetic people. Double up in the summer raining nights or triple up in the cold frigid winters. Body heat was important during the cold months and we had that source of energy. During those loud thunderstorms we had more to hold on to.

Beds came in all forms and creative fashion. We did have the standard twin beds and queen beds. Then we had our beds that were improvised. Unworn cloths were enormous and were piled up on the floor that made large shaped like bean bags. Hampers worked better as a cylinder to play basketball with so we kept the cloths on the floor.

The cloths usually laid around the hamper as a cushion for when we would attempt to slam dunk cloths balls that we tied together. The four foot high by eight foot long collage of fabric also worked wonders as an imitation down feather bed. This was the closest we came to a king size bed.

The living room couch was more popular than the beds. The space was limited, however no elbows or bad breathe to deal with. The mornings were always early if one chose to sleep on the brown burlap spring filled sofa.

Home Grown Wisdom

We had early risers to afternoon slumber bums. The first person to wake up usually would wake the person on the couch and tell them go upstairs if they wanted to continue to sleep.

Sleeping arrangements in the summer always was a treat. The room was endless with the sounds of nature as sleeping outside was an option. There were some situations that prevented us from sleeping outside. The thunderstorms and heavy winds usually would take its toll on our make shift tents.

If we knew it wouldn't rain the best tents were blankets draped over a clothes line and spiked in the ground with wooden clothes pins. We also could sleep on our front covered porch if it did rain.

We also had another options in the summer and that was the place we called our little house. Approximately fifty yards from the house in our back yard was a combination garage and storage place. It was quite large however I never seen a car parked in there. Mostly we had dog cages and rabbit cages and cages for whatever animal we thought needed a cage.

Home Grown Wisdom

The little house was our big play house. Sleeping in there was the best. The rafters were always the place of choice. Since we had carpenter blood in us, anyone of us could build anything. We had those rafters covered with crawl spaces and large areas to relax on. We thought of the little house as our penthouse.

Below the rafters was an area we used for the cages and then there was one room sectioned off as if it was made for a living quarters. There was always a stray mattress or two on the floor. It served the purpose of a couch or bed in many instances.

This was our pow-wow room. It was also a room to hide the friends our parents wouldn't allow us to associate with. It had an easy escape route to the rafters for when we would get surprise visits.

Times in this room were always adventurous and hold many unique memories. The settings created unique situation that often took its own creative paths. The adjacent area with cages, also stored things like paint, lawnmowers, gardening tools etc. etc.

Home Grown Wisdom

I don't think we ever got bored when we were in the little house. Just walking in the garage area was all one needed to do to find entertainment. It was roomy enough to play dodge ball or even basketball.

When we would go on adventures, like ridding one of the worn out mattress down the flooded raging creek that flows at the end of our property, the best place to dry off was in our trusty little house. If you were totally worn out you could just take a nap there also.

We were constantly outside and busy. Climbing the apple tree where Luba and Melon, (names of our neighbors several homes away) lived was not only daring but supplied us with vitamins from those yellow delicious apples.

Melon would often catch us taking his apples and would chase us with a stick. He would yell at us with his foreign accent, "Get out of home, get out of home!"

Putting objects like soda cans or coins on the train tracks was often interesting to watch. We were often curious of how the train would smash certain objects. We could have been responsible for one or two train derailments.

    Making lollipops out of mud and passing them off to an impressionable person named Dolly was one squeamish situation. We also road our bikes through a neighbor's yard that forbid anyone from even walking through it, caused excitement for us. Throwing water on our side walks in the winter gave us a place to slide around. Going to Bower's little corner store to get penny candy was the crown jewel in most of our childhood life.

    Sleeping outside were always the best way to top off any days adventures. Most of us could just sleep out in the open air with nothing more than a blanket beneath us.

    We had tree cabins to sleep in also that were always creative in their own rights. They were always built with fine workmanship. Proper doors and shingled roofs and flower gardens to accent our cabins were always a must. We made the best of everything around us whether it was right or wrong.

Home Grown Wisdom

If the mosquitos were biting on a certain night and the cabins couldn't protect us, we often resorted to sleeping close to the creek. If you kept getting bit you would jump in the creek for a moon light swim. This would usually cool your body down so the mosquitos would stop biting.

Being by the creek in the summer, whether we were sleeping there or having a pool party, was the highlight of our summers.

Sleeping in cars was a popular place when the tents, cabins, little house or open air wasn't an option. We slept in many different styles of cars from junked to new cars.

One neighbor's family had a station wagon. We often slept twelve kids in there on any given evening. Half of those kids would be from our family and the other half from their family. We often thought of the place where we slept as a home base. We often did a lot of roaming in the nights until we needed the base to crash out in.

Sleeping twelve in a car often was crowded, however both families were used to it. This neighboring family also was large with a count of seven. Oddly enough they matched ages with the youngest part of our family even in that gender.

These two families combined were very creative when it came to places to play and places to sleep. We used Train box cars, tops of roofs, inside the middle school and in houses that were up for sale.

All of these previous situations were played out with the third generation of our family. The first generation of our family moved away at young age. Several brothers enlisted in the military, (brother John fought in the Vietnam War), some got married, but we often seen each other when they came back to visit.

Although the younger generation of our family had interesting places to sleep, the older generation had similar stories. Brother Pete fell asleep at a red light in his car for most of a night. He said the red light was to long so he put the car in park and dozed off.

Brother Yonk loved to take a blanket in the open night air and gaze at the stars. Yonk many years later after moving from this two bedroom house came home from California and asked me to sleep outside in the open air with just a blanket. I believe that was the greatest sleep out I ever had.

My father could sleep on a drop of a dime any place anytime. We remember this with a bad taste in our mouths. He could do this mostly because he was often drunk and would only pass out where he ended up.

Pop was also very vocal with body noises while he slept. Snoring meant that he was asleep and we could go about our business. Pop was a sound sleeper with no pun intended.

I guess we all learned to be sound sleepers with all the events going on through many hours of the nights and mornings. We (mostly the last decade group) would often have to pretend we were sleeping while the older kids were down in the living room entertaining. If we would complain to mom the second and third decade group would find out and make us go to bed earlier the next time they had friends over.

Home Grown Wisdom

My sister Amelia, (Lubie), often had her friends sleep over the house. Our family wouldn't be the same if her friends weren't a part of our lives. Cindy from a nearby town and Nicky and Joy from next door and of course Carol, (Killer), was our extended family. They would lie in bed after staying up late at night. They would often yell for us in the morning or we just gravitated to them because we loved them dearly. "Go down and light my cigarette on the stove." Cindy often told me. We would bring up her lit cigarette and a rolling pin. We used the rolling pin to give her a message.

We were far from being financially stable during our early years but we had an exciting life and we probably didn't appreciate it. I wouldn't change any of it for the world. The strange discipline turned out for the good. I feel I learned how to be patient and thankful for having more than one brother or sister. I learned that you had to be an individual in all this mass of hysteria. We learned that there was a bond that grew in the last decade group that will be with us forever.

Home Grown Wisdom

Although we all haven't learned the same values of life growing up together, we all have our own memories that we cherish. We all grew up as individuals and somehow became incompatible.

Wisdom Learned:

Kids are kids, and with little supervision they can be bad kids and at times we were, but we often used wisdom to keep our lives away from danger. We had one brother that absorbed all the jail time when it could have been any one of us. His wisdom came late in life but he gave us more than enough wisdom for what we watched him go through.

The radical fun childhood living in a two bedroom house became a source of remembered do's and don'ts as we grew up. The wisdom learned was spread out over time as we all grew up to be respectful citizens.

A regrettable thought of little combined wisdom learned throughout the family falls short on all of us understanding what we throw away each day, and that is each other. Who has the strength and wisdom to make a change?

A cherished learned wisdom is to choose to never forget the love you got whether it is from your family or friends.

Janet Bojanac Senior: "The secret to life is live, laugh and love." "Do not judge or criticize anyone."

Shared Wisdom

"I learned in life that there is a constant crime against humanity." Lisa spoke in a soft depressed voice. "The government makes more problems for us than we should be allowed to deal with." "Every big business is protected by the laws the government puts out and therefore you and I are always sequestered."

"I can go on and on and give many examples of ignorance in every establishment that surrounds us, but I won't." Lisa kept talking. "I want to keep talking about the injustice that holds our hands behind our backs but I don't want to be depressed today."

"Yes I did gain wisdom from all of this but I'm often reminded to late, to use it."

"Wisdom is, for me anyways, is stop wasting my time trying to do the right thing by shutting up, just be this angry person that somehow lives in me and find peace with that."

Mom

Home Grown Wisdom is mom.

Gretha Bojanac was a pioneer and an adventurer whom moved to America from Oldenburg, Germany in 1941. She left from Germany when she was 28 years old.

She left behind a country that was left in carnage from the allied bombings from WWII. She also left behind the place that sent her to a labor camp at a young age because she born a child to a Yugoslavian man. The Nazi's forbid any German to engage in any way with foreigners.

Gretha spent many months in this labor camp during World War II, when Hitler was in control. The Americans and their allies with their relentless bombing demolished Germany and Hitler. The bombings ended the war and that was when Gretha was freed from the labor camp. Gretha traveled across Germany on foot for fourteen days to find her home.

While traveling across Germany she stayed with farmers and they helped her and guided her in the right direction. "There were no bridges, sometimes an American soldier would help me get across the water." Gretha said. "They were so big and good to me."

Gretha arrived home to find her daughter Kathe still living with her grandmother Katherina and Grandpa Andrew. The man Gretha had her first baby with (Stephanponick), was sent back to his own country, Yugoslavia, while Gretha was in the labor camp.

Gretha then married a man from Yugoslavia named Daniel, (Dueshan) Bojanac. Daniel was a prisoner of Germany and was kept near the farm land where Gretha grew up.

They had four more kids before deciding to move away from the country that couldn't offer them much because the war demolished mostly everything around them.

Home Grown Wisdom

Before they headed off to America they had to endure the loss of one of their children. Pete survived nine months on earth and the cause of death is still unknown. Pete is buried a few kilometers from the house Gretha grew up in.

The family headed to America by boat with the children, Kathe, Paul, John and Pete. (They named the next child Pete after Pete passed). They went through the customary routine that immigrants went through in New York City. They arrived at Ellis Island in 1951.

After moving to Pennsylvania the family grew in number. Gretha and Daniel had a total of thirteen children. Being a mother of one or two children is a job in itself but raising thirteen children in a new country where everything was foreign had to be trying.

With at least three generation gaps in just the kid's lives played an enormous conundrum in trying to raise each child separately.

Home Grown Wisdom played an important role in raising this many kids. I can only speak for myself. My mother first learned who I was and then raised me accordingly. Gretha had a different relationship with each child. I figure she became aware of who they were and treated them as the human being they become.

Gretha had a keen insight on people and seldom wasted time on foolish behaviors or attitudes. "Don't ever crawl them in the ass." Mom used to tell me when I would tell her a brother or a sister wasn't talking to me or treating me with ignorance.

Gretha was always there for support. I don't remember very many or any hugs while growing up except when I ran to her after being hurt. Most of my hugs came late in life. I loved my mom so much for all the **Home Grown Wisdom** she gave me that I often found myself always touching and hugging her. She was my real life angel.

Again, we both grew into learning about each other as time went by and we learned that we had respect for each other without ever saying it.

Gretha was perfect for me, but she must have gotten that way from looking after the older brothers and sisters. Gretha's wisdom knew that each child was different and had strong personalities so each child was raised differently. She admitted that she did what she could do and fell short of guidance to some children.

She also told me that each child grew up being who god set them on earth to be.

Gretha endured more than most people could handle in a life time. With all that surrounded her she always was fun and loving. There wasn't a day where I didn't hear her singing. Mostly songs from Germany and mostly songs from a singer called Engelbert Humpledick.

Gretha was the keystone to the family's existence.

Gretha, working on the farms in Germany

Gretha returned to Germany to visit after 40 years. She couldn't have been happier in life as when she had that chance to visit her home country after all those years.

"My God, it was so beautiful." Gretha said. "I couldn't believe how beautiful it was."

Gretha got this chance to see her younger brother Ludwik and her sister Christina and their children. She also spent time with old childhood friends. They road bicycle's on the roads that she road on as a kid.

Gretha with her brother **Ludwik** and her sister **Christina** after forty years of not seeing each other

Home Grown Wisdom

Gretha was the center piece of all her children's life. She struggled with some but I believe it never lost her much sleep because of the religious wisdom she adopted about all her kids.

Gretha held the family together in her own way. She didn't go out of her way and invite you to her home; you just gravitated there because we loved this woman so much.

When the family would see each other at Gretha's house the family would make attempts to spend more time together during another day. Most of the time it happened, but then there was too many times it did not.

Gretha told me that everybody already made their minds up about everybody else. Your own brothers don't have to like you but they do love you. Just don't beat yourself up, live a happy life with or without your brothers or sisters.

I don't think she gave that speech to each child but I believed she accepted that wisdom over the years she raised her previous kids. I just happen to be near the end of the line, but was lucky enough to understand her wisdom on life.

When Gretha passed away I lost my best friend. Each of her children lost something special. And now there isn't that common place the family can share and could call home.

Wisdom Learned here:

Respect your elders even if you don't understand their ways and appreciate them before it's too late. Listen to their wisdom but only adopt it if they suit your way of life.

If you want to get over being judged then make an effort to change it, or just leave it alone. Don't crawl anybody in the ass unless they are worth it. Decide if family is worth the effort to reach out to, before it's too late. Do things when everybody can still walk and talk with each other, but don't stress if it doesn't happen.

Learn what it means to look outside the box, then look at the box that is you and analyze who you are and change what you can.

Shared Wisdom

"I live day to day and paycheck to paycheck." Monica said. "I got caught up with trying to make things happen fast, but when you do that, you waste money and that's when each day becomes a struggle to get through."

"I use to have a lot of money in the bank and think twice before I bought something or did things that cost money." She kept talking. "Every time I would build up a lot of money something would happen, like a medical problem or somebody would borrow it or something needed repaired and I would lose it all."

"Now that I live day to day, I seem to have more fun with the risk I take every time I have money, but feel depressed when I run out of money."

"Living this way I've learned that it's better to have fun in life than trying to make a rainy day more fun." "The rainy days suck regardless and they happen a lot so just accept them as they come as you should accept everything else in life."

Driving School Kids

Features: K-Kids

(Shit in my hair)

"She put shit in my hair!" Carol began telling the story about one of her bus trips. "This student shit all over herself while she was riding home on the school bus." "I drove to her drop off point and put on some protective gloves and I began to help her get off the bus."

"I got her off the bus with shit all over her." Carol continued her story. "She rubbed it all over herself as if she was playing in it." "She stunk and the bus stunk."

"I put her on the sidewalk and told her mother to take her away; and that was when I took off my gloves and touched my hair." "This little bitch must have rubbed shit in my hair while I bent over beside her."

"I told her about it and she told me that she had brain problems."

"Can I drive tomorrow Mr. Dave?" Darrell asks me every day. "You know I will crash this bus into a tree because these kids drive me crazy the way they scream all the time."

"I'm in front of the police department right now." "Get me help now." Bus 309 yelled over the two-way radio. "I am on the phone with 911 right now." Dispatch told the driver. "This person from 911 is special if you know what I mean, so you have to hold on."

"I'm serious, I need help now, just send them outside, I'm sitting right in front of the police station." The driver demanded. "I've been blowing my horn, I know they can hear me but they won't come outside."

This conversation between the bus driver and dispatch and 911 lasted exactly ten minutes. "Please hold on, the police said they would be outside in a minute." Dispatch concluded. "They will be out after they eat their donuts." Another bus driver that was monitoring the situation as I was on the two-way radio chimed in.

"I have to stay here; the paramedics are on their way." "Please don't let these two kids ride my bus anymore." The bus driver said in a scared voice. "I'm calling the school board now." Dispatch told her.

That afternoon the bus driver that transported those kids to the police department said, "You should have put this story in your book; that kid got beat so bad." "The kid had Timberlake's on and he kept kicking the other kid in the head."

"I couldn't go back there and help him so I drove right to the police station that was on my way." "I hit that horn forever; traffic was backed up but that kid needed help." "The police were right inside the building and they took forever to get out to my bus."

Home Grown Wisdom

"The paramedics came and took one kid; his head was swollen and bloody." "This is just crazy."

While all of this drama was unfolding over the two-way radio I was dealing with problems of my own.

Prior to this day I wrote up a child for wrestling and running in the isle way of the bus. The principal called the parent and informed her that her child would be suspended from the bus.

The next morning while picking up her four other boys that she has, the parent yelled for me to hold on a second. I held the door open and she ran to the bus. I held my hand on the door close switch for a quick close of the door if needed and ultimately safety reasons.

"You pulled away before my little munchkins could sit down." The parent yelled at me. "Thank you and have a great day mam." I replied. "What the hell is your problem, don't drive off with my children still standing!" She added.

I had a short temper this morning because I was listening to my co-worker having to deal with her problems with the fight on her bus. It brought back bad memories of the ignorance of trying to get help but can't when dealing with kids.

Home Grown Wisdom

"Are you serious, you have to do better than that?" I asked the parent. "I'm sure you'll try your hardest to get me fired because I wrote up your son." "Remember we have cameras and a zonar system on our bus, so be careful of what you try to do."

"I know how to deal with people like you Mr. Dave, so be careful of what you do and be careful of how you deal with my son's." The parent told me in a low voice while steering at me intently.

I started to close the door and she told me that she won't tolerate me writing up her son's in the future. "Please don't try to intimidate me mam." "You now ruined my day, so step away from the bus."

This parent questioned the principal regarding me driving while the kids were standing in the isle way. He told me they watched the video tape and never seen anyone standing while I was driving. He also told me he witnessed the kids wrestling.

After the principal called the parent with his findings the parent met me at the bus stop the next morning. "What did I tell you…?" She tried to yell at me but I closed the door in her face and drove away.

Home Grown Wisdom

"My mom said Your Fired, Mr. Dave." A K-kid told me. "Mommy told me to keep standing in the isle so you will get fired." "You tell your mommy she's beautiful." I told the K-Kid.

"I went home after my morning runs and watched the TV show COPS and tried to take a nap." Bus Driver Betty said. "That song bad boy, bad boy, what you gonna do, started and it was like they were right near my house because I thought I heard real gun shots."

"I later went back to work and drove to my high school for my afternoon run and was stopped at the school's entry because they had a lock down." "Only a few kids were allowed to drive home with me." The bus driver kept talking.

"Kids were crying getting on the bus." "They told me that their friend was shot and killed on the north side." Bus driver Betty then found out that her neighbor was the kid who was killed and the gun shots that she thought was on COPs was actually real gun shots.

"Mr. Dave, Mr. Dave, He's pre-verted, cause he's acting like he's having a baby." One K-Kid yelled. "No, you fool, he's inverted." Another kid said. "You all dumb, its pervited." One last kid said.

"Who are they going to believe?" "Me, and outstanding teacher, or you, a young punk that is always in trouble?" A teacher told a child on my bus. "Look at me, get your act together now." "See me in the morning; we got some things to work out."

The new principal came on the bus during this conversation between the teacher and the student. "Look at me; you will stay in your seat and you will not hit another child or else you will be off the bus." The principal said in his soft voice.

Our bus held up the other busses from leaving that day because I wrote up ten kids and each child had to be addressed by the three different teachers and one principal that boarded the bus. "I laid down the law, so I don't think you'll have any more problems." The new principal said.

"I need the school police; these kids are fighting and throwing things." I said over the two-way radio two minutes after I pulled away from the school.

"Mr. Dave, DeeDee kissed Leaona on the lips." One K-kid said. "She's a lesbian." "She's too little to be a lesbian." "You don't turn into a lesbian until you go to high school." Another K-Kid concluded.

Home Grown Wisdom

"I had no choice I had to back up." A bus driver started talking over the two-way radio. "There were police everywhere and I drove between them down this road and they stopped me and told me I couldn't proceed." "I backed into a car, I had no choice, I had to back up, there was no way out, I had to back up."

"Let me reiterate the backup policy that is strictly enforced." Safety manager said over the two-way radio. "Nobody is permitted to back up without assistance except for backing in the bus lot."

"A car swerved into my lane and hit the side of the bus." Another bus driver came over the two-way radio only a few minutes later.

Minutes after that radio transmission anther bus driver said, "My mirrors are damaged; the beam on the bridge knocked them off." "Please, take your time and observe you're surroundings." "You are a professional driver." Safety said over the two-way radio. "Please, take your time and drive professionally."

With all the strick rules and regulation about being in accidents on the bus, not one person was suspended or fired. School bus drivers are extremely hard to find because of the evil you have to deal with on a daily basis so I guess they get away with a lot more than they should.

"Shut up, shut up, shut up!" "Dang, I never cussed so much in my life." One K-Kid yelled. "These dang kids; sorry Mr. Dave for my bad mouth but I've had it."

"I read your book Driving School Kids Dave, you really had some tuff times." Another bus driver told me one morning. "I'm not sure how to handle what you went through."

"Dispatch, could you call the principal to meet my bus?" "I have a fight on the bus and the kids will not sit down." That same bus driver

Home Grown Wisdom

whom told me that he didn't have the problems I had, transmitted problem after problem that whole day.

When I seen him that afternoon I asked him if he would share any stories that I could use in my next book. "Well Dave, I just have fights now and then and kids standing in their seats and an occasional curse word thrown my way." The Bus driver told me. "I just have these basic stories: nothing out of the ordinary to write about."

"I don't have kids having sex on the bus or kids getting shot at; but when I do I'll let you know." "I do get stopped by irate parents a lot but you covered that in your last book."

"Why were you absent yesterday Mr. Dave?" A K-Kid asked me. "I had to set that fat lady straight." "She went the wrong way and she drove like a crazy women; and I ain't gonna have that."

"I wish I could retire; these damn kids threw food at me the whole way home." "What the hell." "I wrote up the whole bus." A bus driver told me. "They know if they get written up, they could go back to jeuvinille hall; but they just don't think."

On that afternoon the crys of this frustrated driver sounded off over the two-way radio. "Damn it, I've had it." "I've been hit with french fries all morning and now these kids are spraying water on me with squirt guns."

That afternoon while chatting in the break room with this driver she told me that she was written up by management for getting the kids late to school. "I got hit with fries and sprayed with water and I get written up."

"You know Dave, I'm gonna retire early." "If I hear or see one more child that has no respect for adults I might just kill them, so I think I've come to my breaking point." This wonderful softspoken bus driver quit driving that very next day.

 "Mr. Dave, do you have some candy?" "I'm going to tell on you if you don't give me some candy." A K-Kid told me. "You know you'll be fired, so give me some candy."

"The school police are on their way, so do not move that bus." Dispatch said over the two-way radio.

On this particular bus run I had seventeen kids on board the bus and two of my favorite kids turned against me for some odd reason.

"Sit down and quit mocking me." I said after a few minutes of trying to control these two girls rully behavior. "Sit down and quit mocking me." The two girls kept saying. "You know I called the police on you." I said. "You know I called the police on you." They continued to mock me.

Home Grown Wisdom

While we waited for nearly an hour the kids called their parents to pick them up. I let all the kids go that had parents show up except for the two girls. "Let me off the bus now." "I hate you." "I did nothing wrong." "I hate you." They kept yelling as they tried to push the door open to exit the bus.

The school police came and they both cried like they were going to jail. "I don't know what his problem is..." The girls tried to tell the police. "I'm not enterested in anything you have to say so shut up now." The police told the girls as they took them to the police car.

"Mr. Dave, I found a dead raccoon on the street and took him home." A K-Kid told me. "I'm gonna put a pillow in him when he dries up and give him to my baby sister for her birthday."

Home Grown Wisdom

On this one of particular day dispatch was flooded with problems over the two-way radio.

The first problem, "A kid just dropped a knife while exiting the bus." "The crossing guard grabbed it from him so I need an incident report made out."

The second problem, "A parent drove in front of my moving bus to stop me." "She is now standing at my door but I ain't gonna open it." "I have no idea who she is."

The third problem, "Dispatch, I am pulling up to my first stop and I see the parent of that child I wrote up." "I told you she would be there; I'm going to drive on by." "Somebody else can deal with this crazy lady."

The fourth problem, "They're out of control, they're out of control." "I'm pulling this bus over until they sit down and quit screaming." Another frustated bus driver said. "When you get back to the lot I need to see you." Dispatch told the driver. "You got to give this run to somebody else, these kids are crazy." The bus driver concluded.

"Go faster, Go faster, Go faster, Go faster, Go faster, Go faster, Go faster, Go faster, Go faster, Go faster, Go faster, Go faster, Go faster, Go faster, Go faster, Go faster, Go faster, Go faster." The K-Kids yelled.

I am just so pissed off with a parent of a kid that I drive to school. This parent is at my pick up spot every morning. This is the third day that this parent stepped on the bus and threatened me.

"I had no problem with you, but now I will be your biggest problem." She yelled at me. "Don't you ever yell at my kid!"

When I told her to back away and that she was breaking the law by standing on a school bus she again threatened me. I told her that I was closing the door and started to pull it shut when she got off the bus. She told my boss that the door hit her bussoms.

This parents motive for attacking me was that I wrote her son up for standing and hanging out the window. Prior to this I told the principal and two different teachers that this child was out of control and I needed there help.

I also told them that I did not want to write this child up because this parent gestures to me daily with a fist pump or a middle finger daily.

When the principal and the teachers told me that I would have to write that child up because they needed a paper trail to add to their papers they already have, I got nervous.

Two days went by after I aggreed to write this child up. I was hoping everybody would forget about my promise to write this child up, but they didn't. I was also asked to pull the video tape to back up our accusations. These people of authority must of new what would happen if this particular parent got upset with her child being disciplined by somebody other than her.

The parent was called by the principal one morning and that afternoon that parent started her rage against me. Her body lanquage was frightening, like a stare down and her hands on her hips was first noticed, but that was enough, I knew what would be coming next.

The next morning she held her kids up and then slowly walked them to the bus. She tired their shoes, wiped their faces and zipped their coats. I turned off my eight way flashing lights and just sat there. I didn't show any frustration because I knew that was what she wanted.

The next morning she sat in the car until all the other kids were borded and then yelled for me to wait. Again I waited and showed no frustration, but was getting very anoid.

Home Grown Wisdom

The third day she ran to the bus in front of her kids. She held her hand high on the door to let kid after kid onto the bus. The last child got on and she did to. "What did I tell you about...?" The parent tried to say something

"Mam, you are breaking the law, please get off the bus." I interupted her statement. "If you have a problem call my boss and they will pull the video tape and prove your wrong agian, so please step off the bus."

The parent started yelling at me so I keyed the two-way radio microphone so my boss and dispatch could hear how this parent was yelling at me. When the parent was done verbally assulting me, I did what I promised I would never do again and that was confront a parent.

"You know that your playing these games because a bus driver wrote you child up." I told her. "You know that your child was warned by me and the teachers at the school that your child is out of control." "We were looking for your help to deal with the problem but you didn't." " Nobody wanted to write up your child because we felt you would act this way."

"Now I am your worst nightmare!" The parent turned and stared at me with an intense look. " I will take care of you and you will not be driving busses ever again." "Promises, Promises." I had to through my last comment in before she ended with her last words.

I drove away and was angry that I fell into her trap. I accidently expressed my frustration. Now that it is done I wish I would have thrown in some curse words that I hear all the time from parents.

I am spent with frustration and will never know how I lasted these last few years dealing with crazy parents.

This parent called the company and admitted she got on the bus. Now the company has her admission that she was on the bus and also heard her verbally assult me over the two-way radio. With all this information nothing was done. I was actually told by safety that she was out to get you and I was out to get her, and with that weak analysis we had to let things go.

With this lack of effort in dealing with parents that I've seen time and time again raised my blood pressure ten fold. When I was told I was out to get her was the breaking point. At that point I new I was done. I will never fight the fight again.

The school was still dealing with this parent. The principal asked to view the bus video tape. He later told me he seen nothing out of the ordinary that would cause and alarm of unsafe driving while kids were standing or sitting. He told me he discussed this with the parent and the parent changed the subject and said I slammed the door on her bussoms.

I can't laugh at this point but someday I will. Not only did the principal tell me what this crazy parent said; I then learned from my safty manager that the parent told him that she wanted and apology for having her bussums slammed in the bus door.

"Mr. Dave, why did you yell at that parent?" A K-Kid asked while jumping up and down. "If that was me, I would have kicked her in her nasty mouth." "Mr. Dave, don't take crap from that nasty lady."

You can't keep a low profile when you are a bus driver. You are in the public eye and parents are constantly reporting every move you make. You can be as nice a person anybody would ever imagine you could be, and I tried, but it is just a waste of time. Nobody ever notices.

When dealing with fellow employes is also difficult. Each day is different, you never know what you'll fall into when you open your mouth to talk. You might fall into something good and then you most likely fall into something bad.

Home Grown Wisdom

Since I published the book called **Driving School Kids** I had to promote the book to fellow bus drivers. I posted an order form on the bulletin board, and never verbally asked anybody to order my book. I joked with my closest friends to get a copy of the book but had no pressure sales.

I got a lot of feed back from a lot of drivers, one driver came back to me with concern. "David, if I didn't know you and read this book, I would think you were racist." That statement from a close friend made my knee's weak.

As she began to open the book I started a nervous chuckle because that was the last thing I thought I would hear from a friend who wanted to write a book together on racism.

"Here, read this and tell me what you meant." She told me while handing me the book I wrote that she highlighted with a yellow marker. "Black people would be offended if they read this, so tell me how you could write this?"

Home Grown Wisdom

"WOW!" I said out loud. "Are you serious?" "Do you think I'm talking about black people here?" "WOW." I was beside myself thinking this friend is trying to paint me as a racist. "I hate to tell you this." I told her. "These three little girls live on Chartiers Avenue and not one of them are black." "How did you ever paint these kids black."

"Well, you talked about poverty and you mentioned you were a white bus driver so it is clear all these problems in this book is about a white bus driver dealing with black folks."

"Now I see who is not only a racist but prejudice." I told her. "Of all people that I know, and all the time we spent together, you misread everything I wrote and drew your own conclusion of what was written or not written."

I didn't see this person for a few days after that but when I did I asked if I could have one final minute trying to understand what she misunderstood or misread. I thought maybe I could learn something but I was wrong.

Home Grown Wisdom

Prior to me asking her to talk I was stopped by another bus driver. He told me, a friend of mine is going around showing your book and all the things she highlighted. She's saying if she didn't know you, she would thing you were a racist.

I ran to her and stopped her from getting in her car and demanded and explanation. "I never showed anybody but you David, I swear." She told me. In her second breath she said she only showed dispatch. "If you only showed me and dispatch then how and why is everybody talking about it?" I asked her.

The situation was intense and I just told her we were done and that I lost all respect for her. She started crying and told me she was going to go to management and get me fired.

I walked along side her and we argued back and fouth and I was dumbfounded that she made every effort to paint me as a racist.

In the managers office I let her talk until I thought she was done. I took mental notes to all the gafs that I would use to prove that she was a liar and a person that was out to hurt a fellow co-worker. You see, I became good at this type of defense because I dealt with many lying parents and kids in the past few years as a school bus driver.

This person would not let me talk, she kept saying oh my god David over and over again. I got so annoyed by it I told her to shut up and show some respect. After I proved my case she turned away and gave up. She was defeated yet I felt the same.

I hugged her and whispered in her ear. "You are no longer a friend, good-bye. Two days later she quit her job. The rumor mill started up immediately that she quit because of David.

"Mr. Dave; why do you look so sad today?" A K-Kid asked me. "You got a sad face like somebody got shot, or you might be missing somebody." "Am I right Mr. Dave?" "Answer me bald headed bus driver."

Home Grown Wisdom

"I dropped Tony, (an Eighth grade special need student) right in front of his home. " Edna began to tell a story of a missing boy. "I saw his dad in the door waiting for him." "Tony opened the gate to the yard and I drove off. That evening the FBI and the police were looking for him."

"What else can I do?" Edna asked. "After I dropped him off I did seen him walk towards the corner store, and his dad seen him walk that way also."

"I didn't see him at his stop that next morning so I thought he was still missing." Edna said. "I was real nervous at that point." "Then at the last stop for that school that morning there was Tony at the wrong bus stop."

"You know the FBI and police are looking for you because you didn't go home last night." Tony curled up in his seat as if he was scared of what might happen next.

"This job is crazy." "We have to drive kids that give us a hard time all day and then we have days like this where we have to worry about them all night." Edna concluded.

"Mr. Dave, I like you today." Naimi told me. "Do you have any gum?" "No I don't." I replied. "Then why did I waste my time saying I like you?" Naimi concluded.

What a funny bunch of kids. Every morning I have the pleasure to verbally chat with some young bright funny kids on one of my bus runs. OMG, is a constant. They keep me up to date on the latest trends and music. When I try to teach them about the past I get OMG. (Oh My God)

Driving can be quite boring especially when you sit in city traffic. I often listen to the conversations going on and take a quick look to see what the kids are up to, as I watch them through the oversized rearview mirror.

Every day we have fun talking and joking but this one day the full moon was obviously out because everybody on the bus took their creative juices to the extreme and acted quite bazar.

"Ching, Chang, Hung." Lizzy yelled out the bus window at a Chinese man walking down the sidewalk. "Get a car!" Baily, Lizzy and Daisha yelled at a group of people that were waiting at a port authority bus stop.

While all of this was going on I looked in the oversized mirror and watch a kid named Zane put an elastic glove over his head. I recommend he pull it down past his nose and blow it up that way.

After filling the fingers up with air that was at the top of his head another kid named Luke tried to eliminate the air from each figure except the middle finger. Zane walked to the back of the bus and the girls that sat in the front rows continued their yells at pedestrians along the bus route.

Sometimes as a bus driver you have to see how far a group of kids will go if you let them do what they want. I did keep a close watch and made sure everything they did was safe.

I knew I couldn't let them continue this each bus trip so I had to come up with a plan to stop them. I didn't want to write them up because I was to blame for letting them get somewhat out of control.

I should have respected them enough to just tell them they couldn't stand on the bus or yell out the window but I chose to be creative in my correction process. I told the kids the people that they yelled at called my boss and told my boss how they yelled at them and a description of each of them.

This was obvious a lie but it worked, and why did I handle it this way because I know that right about now, after reading what I just wrote, Baily and Telesha and Daisha and Lizzy are saying OMG.

Home Grown Wisdom

"Mr. Dave, he showed me the middle finger." Suzy told me after she yelled out the window. "Are you my daddy?" "I need some money." "Are you my daddy?"

I deal with racism just like the next person does. I hear blacks discriminate and play the race card on whites and I hear whites discriminated and play the race card on blacks.

Racism is everywhere. Prejudice is everywhere. Jealousy is everywhere. Ignorance is everywhere and is the catalyst for all that is wrong in society. We as human beings will remain ignorant forever and all things associated with it will also remain that way.

When I hear or see racism on my bus I refuse to remain ignorant, and yes I get myself into hot spots quiet often.

Home Grown Wisdom

I drive for this one school that has kids that are more sophisticated and smarter than most of the other city schools. This doesn't say they don't have their share of ignorance.

I got to know these kids through conversations we would have driving to and from school and they became trusting with me and shared a lot of stories I wish I never listened to.

This one white boy who was popular with all the other students and whom I also became popular with had friends ride home with him one afternoon on the bus.

"Dave, these kids that are new to the bus are in the back saying I can't sit in the back of the bus because I was white." One girl whispered my way. I asked her get the other girls from the back and come talk with me.

"They told me it was ok for me to stay back there because I was black." Another girl told me. They told me who was saying this and I immediately felt obligated to do something about it.

After dealing with this ignorance many times before in all different areas I knew I couldn't deal with it anymore. I had to pass the buck to a school official.

I reported the incident and waited a few days until I asked the girls did they say anything to the school official. The girls told me that they were all disgusted because nothing can be done to those boys because their parents work in the school system.

I told the kids welcome to my world.

Wisdom Learned:

I didn't try hard enough to find another job. I also learned that it never pays to confront a parent, good or bad, even if the kid is great most of the time. The precious little darlings are just precious for a short period of time then they grow into being the parents that raised them.

Just an observation:

Here is a nursery rhyme. A lot of times we don't comprehend what we read. Just read it and ask yourself what does it mean and could you gain any wisdom from it?

> **Hush a bye baby, on the tree top,**
> **when the wind blows the cradle will rock;**
> **when the bow breaks, the cradle will fall,**
> **and down will come baby, cradle and all.**

Wisdom gained: Don't put your baby in a tree when it's windy.

Commercial:

Don't make this the last book you read written by David Bojanac. Make shore you read the crazily funny book called, "Scoop the Poop." "Scoop the Poop is one of those books you might feel weird about reading because it deals with poop, but you won't regret it.

Scoop the Poop is way beyond the subject of poop; it has human interest stories that were shared by many people of all class types. Do yourself a favor and give it a try: Also a great stocking stuffer.

Driving School Kids is 182 pages of excitement when it deals with kids, parents, teachers and everybody associated with kids. Unbelievable true stories that are gut wrenching to totally hilarious.

Have fun reading **Driving School Kids**. Driving School kids II is part of this book because I had to share a few of the stories that came my way after finishing the first book. I also wanted to share the wisdom I learned from Driving School Kids. It's a great book and I hope you read it.

The End

Made in United States
Orlando, FL
09 January 2022